Preface

GW00649733

Fencing has always tended to be seen as a sp[ort]
schools or in the armed forces – this is largel[y]
origins. But although a code of gentlemanly
within the sport, fencing is now more widely offered throughout the country
than ever before and is a popular activity in sports centres, youth clubs and
holiday activity centres.

Fencing clubs exist in most parts of the country, offering classes for all ages and
abilities, men competing equally with women. National championships are held
for all age groups, from the under 11s up to the over 60s.

You're never too young or too old to start foil fencing. To master the sport
properly, it's essential to attend classes or individual sessions with a qualified
fencing coach. That said, it's always useful to have something to refer to in
between coaching sessions to remind you of what you have learnt.

Fencers of all ages and abilities will find this handbook invaluable. Not only will it
help new fencers to understand and remember key foil fencing terms and
techniques, it will also help more experienced fencers to develop and perfect
their foil fencing skills, particularly the training exercises given in Chapter Six.

For ease of understanding, descriptions are kept to a minimum and there are
plenty of illustrations to help you visualise how to perform various fencing
techniques. Key fencing terms appear in bold text the first time they are
introduced and, where appropriate, definitions are given in brackets in italic text.
Don't worry if you don't understand some of the terms used – the glossary at
the back of the handbook contains definitions of over 150 fencing terms.

And it's not just fencers who will benefit from the handbook. Coaches (both
qualified and trainee) will find it a useful aid to teaching key foil fencing
techniques. As well as pointing out what to look out for when assessing fencers'
skills, the handbook also contains useful information on running fencing classes
including class organisation, safety and training exercises.

So whatever your role, whether fencer or coach, and whatever your level of
experience, this compact, easy-to-read handbook is for you.

Contents

Contents

Introduction

Chapter 1

The sport of fencing is a game of physical chess played at lightning speed.

This remark has been attributed to several *Old Masters of the Fence,* so its actual origin is just as clouded as the origins of fencing itself.

However, we do know that the sword is one of the oldest of weapons and that a whole variety of shapes and sizes have been used all over the world throughout history. This chapter takes a brief look at the history of the sword and traces the development of fencing as we know it today.

The Origins of Fencing

One of the earliest examples of the sword in use is shown in Egyptian drawings. These show men fighting with stick-like swords in one hand, with the other arm bound for protection and used for defence.

The Romans used short, dagger-like swords and wore protective leather, thonged clothing.

Later, military swords with heavy broad blades were developed. As the use of protective armour increased, so swords became larger, until two hands were required to wield the mighty weapons.

With the invention of gunpowder, the musket and bayonet largely replaced the sword for military use. Bayonet fencing was practised in all three armed services until recent years. However, cavalry regiments retained swords long after the infantry began to use rifles and bayonets. Swords were particularly efficient for delivering lethal cuts from horseback.

In the 17th and 18th centuries, sword techniques developed to make more use of a thrusting action, using the point rather than the edge of the blade to inflict injury on the adversary. As a result, various designs of rapiers were developed. These had long, tapering blades that finished in a well-honed point, and often had a cup hilt to protect the swordsman's hand.

This in turn led to the development of short swords that were easy to carry and could be used for personal protection. Many of these were richly embellished to match the fashions of the day.

It soon became a necessary social accomplishment for men of good breeding to develop their sword skills. Not only were sword skills an indication of a gentleman's social standing, but, with the increasing trend of duelling to settle matters of honour, they were also essential for continued good health!

Sword techniques were developed and taught by *Masters of the Fence*. In England, Henry VIII granted letters of patent to *Masters of ye Noble Science of Defence*. Although these acknowledged the profession of those who taught sword skills, the profession was never really taken up formally until much later in history. During the 18th century, Domenico Angelo taught fencing at Eton, Winchester and Harrow. In 1763, the first illustrated manual of fencing techniques to be produced in England was published.

Fencing Today

Today, fencing is an Olympic sport and has been included in every Olympic Games since Baron de Coubertin revived the ancient games in 1896.

The modern sport of fencing dates back to the days when swordsmanship was practised with a fencing master. Using a light, flexible sword, fencers were taught to develop their speed and dexterity, and techniques with which to deliver a fatal thrust to an adversary's body. Since they had neither shield nor dagger to use for defence, they had to learn to use their sword to both attack and defend.

Of course, the aim of fencing has changed somewhat since then. Nowadays, fencers score hits rather than deliver fatal blows to their opponent! However, the principles of the sport remain the same. This section gives a brief overview of what fencing is all about. Key fencing terms are highlighted in bold. Don't worry if you don't understand all of them – all will be explained later on. You can also refer to the glossary at the back of the book.

Types of Sword

Three different types of sword are used in modern fencing:

Figure 1: Foil

The **foil** is a light, flexible, thrusting weapon, developed from the traditional small sword. It takes its name from the Old French word for *dulled point.* Valid **hits** are scored by thrusting the point of the foil at the trunk of the opponent's body.

Figure 2: Epée

The **épée** is a modern version of the duelling rapier and is used in the modern pentathlon. The blade has a triangular section. Valid hits are scored by thrusting the point of the épée at the opponent's body, arms, legs and head.

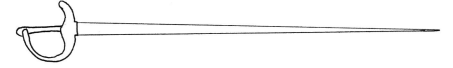

Figure 3: Sabre

The **sabre** is a lighter, more flexible version of the military sabre. Valid hits are scored by using *edge cuts* or *point thrusts* on the opponent's arms, head or body above the waist.

This handbook concentrates on **foil fencing**.

Foil Fencing

Whatever type of sword is used, the aim of fencing is to score as many hits as possible. In foil fencing, hits are only valid if the point of the foil is placed on the opponent's trunk of body **(target area)** with sufficient force, so that if it were a sharp point, it would pierce the flesh. Hits to the arms, legs or head do not count.

The shaded parts of the fencer in Figures 4 and 5 show the target area in foil fencing.

Figure 4: Target area
(front)

Figure 5: Target area
(back)

Either fencer can choose to attack at any time during a **bout** *(fight for a specific number of hits)*. According to fencing rules, an **attack** is *the initial offensive action made by a fencer who is extending the sword arm and continuously threatening the opponent's target.* In other words, an attack involves reaching forwards with the foil to hit the opponent's target area with the point of the foil.

When one fencer chooses to attack *(the attacker)*, the other *(the opponent)* must recognise this as a valid attempt to score a hit and defend by deflecting the oncoming foil point from its intended target with their foil blade **(parry)**.

If, however, the opponent is taken by surprise by the attacker and reacts by hitting back without parrying first, the attacker will score the hit, even if both fencers hit each other at the same time.

Once the opponent has successfully defended against the attack **(parried)**, they can immediately hit back **(riposte)**. This time, the *attacker* must parry.

This exchange of parrying and riposting occurs each time one fencer chooses to attack and continues until one fencer hits the other, on or off target, or the exchange is broken off.

If both fencers choose precisely the same moment to attack each other and they both succeed in hitting, on or off target, neither of them scores the hit. However, if one fencer hits on target and the other misses altogether, the fencer who hits on target will score the hit.

During a bout, trained fencers try to create a moment when they can catch their opponent *off guard* to deliver a successful attack. However, they must always be aware that their opponent may attack and must therefore be ready to defend if necessary. Fencing therefore becomes a test of concentration, tactical awareness, explosive acceleration and immediate actions. As conditions continually change during a bout, fencing is an *open skill* sport.

National and International Fencing

The **Fédération Internationale d'Escrime** (FIE) is the international governing body for fencing. It is responsible for establishing rules of combat and organising World Cup events, World Championships and Olympic fencing competitions.

British Fencing is the national governing body responsible for the development of fencing in the UK. Its main tasks include training new fencing coaches, establishing policies for fencing within the UK, and training and selecting teams for international championships and the Olympic Games.

British Fencing organises a full calendar of events each year. These range from children's competitions to veterans' championships. In addition, the UK hosts a number of FIE World Cup events that attract the best fencers in the world.

British fencers have to qualify for places in the national fencing teams. The teams in turn must achieve good results at World Cup events to qualify for the Olympic Games. The European zone, in which Britain is included, is the strongest world zone in fencing. Many European countries have a long tradition in fencing and fencers from those countries are well funded and attend well-established training centres.

Fencing for Young People

British Fencing runs a national programme of development that offers young people of all ages the opportunity to try fencing. Often, young people who are reluctant to take part in sport find that they enjoy the individuality of fencing, matching their own skill, speed and intellect against those of an opponent, female competing equally with male.

In schools, fencing classes can be held in almost any indoor area with an average ceiling height and non-slip floor. Unlike some sports, fencing is a year-round activity, ideal for wet, cold, winter days when outdoor sports are not so popular. It is included on the GCSE PE syllabus by a number of examination boards and is also included in the Duke of Edinburgh's Award scheme.

Fencing for Disabled People

Many disabilities prove to be of little disadvantage in fencing. In fact, many fencers who are considered disabled compete very successfully in able-bodied competitions – a British fencer with one hand once won the World Championships.

Fencing for wheelchair users is a major sport. The **British Disabled Fencing Association** organises training and selects disabled fencing teams in the UK. Many of the medal winners at recent World Championships and Paralympics have been British disabled fencers.

Chapter 2

Fencing Equipment

Introduction

The protective clothing used for fencing is made to the highest standards and allows fencers to move freely while protecting all parts of the body. Figure 6 below shows fencers in full fencing kit.

Figure 6: Fencing equipment comes in a range of sizes to fit men, women and children

Fencing clubs and beginners' classes will provide all the necessary equipment to start with, but fencers will probably soon want to buy their own. It is usually best to buy one or two items at a time and gradually build up a collection of equipment, which should last for many years.

This chapter starts by listing the basic equipment new fencers will require. It then moves on to additional equipment that fencers may want to acquire and concludes with guidance on storing and maintaining fencing equipment.

Basic Equipment_____

Mask

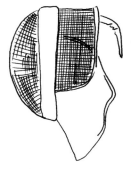

Fencers must **always** wear a **mask** when fencing, particularly to protect their eyes, which can so easily be injured.

Figure 7: Mask

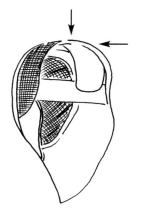

The hook at the back of the fencer's head should be adjusted, so that the mask fits snugly, even when the fencer's head jerks forwards. Some masks are fitted with an additional elastic back strap for extra security.

Figure 8: Adjusting hook

Masks should be checked regularly to make sure they are in good condition and should never be used if they are in any way damaged. The following check-list shows what to look for when inspecting masks.

REMEMBER!

- There should be no signs of rust on the mesh.

- The mesh should not cave inwards when pressed hard with the thumb.

- The bib should be well attached to the mesh and have no gaps or holes.

- When the mask is on, the bib should not curl away from the fencer's neck.

Foil

Most non-electric **foils** are suitable for fencing classes, provided the blades are not broken or badly bent, and the points are flattened and covered with a rubber **button**. Holiday souvenirs from Toledo, however, should be avoided!

Two types of foil are commonly used:

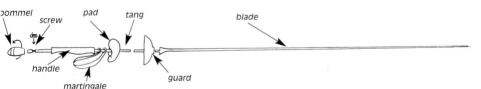

Figure 9: The **French grip foil** *has a straight handle*

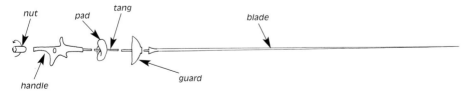

Figure 10: The **orthopaedic grip foil** *has a moulded pistol style grip*

There are left-handed and right-handed versions of both types of foil. Smaller sizes are also available for young fencers.

Figure 11 shows the maximum length and weight of a full-size foil. The blade must deflect by a maximum of 9.5cm when supported 70cm from the point, with a 200-gram weight applied 3cm from the point.

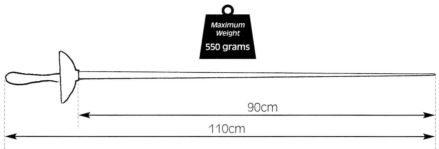

Figure 11: Maximum length and weight of a full-size foil

Jacket

Jackets are made of cotton or synthetic materials that are strong enough to meet the national standards set by British Fencing and come in a range of sizes to fit men, women and children.

Jackets must cover the full target area (see page 4 for further details about the target area). They either fasten at the back (see Figure 12) or on the non-sword arm side (see Figure 13). Those used by fencing classes sometimes have additional straps so that fencers can adjust them to fit.

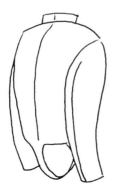

Figure 12: Jacket fastening at the back

Figure 13: Jacket fastening on the non-sword arm side

Women's jackets must have pockets for chest protector plates. These are designed to hold the **individual chest protectors** shown in Figure 14.

Figure 14: Individual chest protectors

Full chest protectors like the one shown in Figure 15 are also available. These are preferable to individual chest protectors as they offer more protection to the chest area.

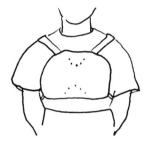

Figure 15: Full chest protector

Glove

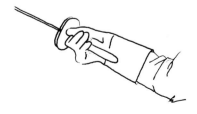

Gloves must be made of material that is strong enough to protect the sword hand. The cuff must be long enough to fit over the sleeve of the jacket and extend halfway between the wrist and the elbow as shown in Figure 16.

Figure 16: Glove

Other Clothing

Apart from the mask, foil, jacket and gloves, new fencers do not necessarily need any other fencing equipment. The following items of ordinary clothing are suitable:

- Shoes – any type of general-purpose sports shoes with light-coloured soles.
- Clothes – a tee shirt and tracksuit bottoms with shorts underneath for added protection. Tight-fitting jeans, shorts on their own or short skirts should be avoided. Otherwise fencing classes might be filled with shrieks of pain if fencers are hit off target, or hoots of laughter at the sound of ripping trousers!

Additional Equipment

Breeches

As with jackets, **breeches** are made of cotton or synthetic materials that are strong enough to meet the national standards set by British Fencing.

Breeches fasten on the non-sword arm side and should extend under the jacket at the waist by at least 10cm. The legs of the breeches should fasten just below the knee. Braces can be worn if preferred.

Figure 17: Breeches

Socks

When wearing breeches, the lower legs must be covered with long, white socks that extend over the knee.

Shoes

Fencing shoes are specially designed so that they are reinforced around the toes and have extra padding around the heels.

Headband

Fencing is an energetic sport and can generate a lot of sweat. Wearing a headband helps prevent sweat impairing fencers' vision.

Care of Equipment

Generally, fencing equipment will last for many years if it is maintained and stored correctly. Equipment used by fencing classes will be suitable for many generations of fencers if it is stored in a cupboard or storage area that is completely damp-free and, if possible, kept warm.

Clothing

Storage
Clothing and gloves get very damp while fencing. They should therefore be stored well away from masks and foil blades to prevent rust forming on the latter.

Maintenance
Clothing should be stored on hangers or loosely laid in plastic baskets to air. It should be laundered regularly and inspected for tears or holes.

Masks

Masks should be stored either in wire baskets or hung on a rail by their hooks. Avoid forcing one mask over another as this will damage the internal padding.

Foils

Foils used by fencing classes should be marked left- or right-handed as appropriate so that they are easy to identify. Lines can also be drawn at the top of the handles to make it easier to teach fencers how to hold the foil correctly.

Storage

Foils should be stored either by:

- laying them down horizontally
- hanging them in a rack, or
- standing them upright with the pommels resting on the floor.

Maintenance

Occasionally, the rubber buttons covering foil points fall off, split or allow the blade to push through. They should always be replaced when this happens.

After they have been used for some time, foil blades can become severely bent or break completely. They must be replaced immediately if there is any doubt as to whether or not they are safe. To do this, the hilt is dismantled by unscrewing the pommel, the old blade removed and the new blade fitted. Care must be taken to mount the handle correctly when reassembling the foil.

chapter 3

Key Techniques

Introduction

This chapter introduces 11 key foil fencing techniques:

- Holding the foil
- Salute
- On Guard
- Steps forwards and backwards
- Scoring a hit
- Lunge
- Guards
- Defence (including the parry and riposte)
- Simple actions
- Compound actions
- Successive parries.

Each subsection that follows includes a brief description of one of the above techniques, accompanying illustration(s) and a list of key points to remember when performing the technique.

This chapter of the handbook is specifically aimed at new fencers and therefore addresses the fencer as *you* throughout. However, coaches of new fencers will find the chapter equally useful. In particular, the lists of key points serve as a useful reminder of what to look out for when assessing fencers' skills.

Holding the Foil_____

The most important technique of all is learning to hold the foil correctly. This is the key to developing accurate foil fencing skills.

When you are holding the foil correctly, you should be able to:

- place the point on your opponent's target area accurately, and
- make the blade bend correctly without using excessive force.

Figure 18 shows how to hold the foil correctly.

When your sword arm is bent at the elbow, there must be a straight line between your elbow and the point of your foil. The foil forms an extension of your forearm.

Figure 18: Holding the foil

REMEMBER!

To hold the foil correctly, remember:

- Thumb on top of the handle close to the cushion.
- Index finger curled under the handle.
- Three fingers on the handle, with the two centre fingers through the martingale.
- Pommel pressing into the centre of the wrist.

Salute

Fencers **salute** each other before crossing swords to acknowledge their respect for their opponent, fencing coach or training partner. The custom of saluting dates back to the chivalrous days of duelling. Figure 19 shows the three main movements that make up the salute.

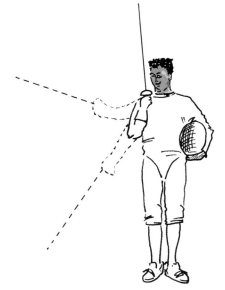

Figure 19: The salute

REMEMBER!

To salute correctly, remember:

- Feet at right angles, heels touching.
- Legs straight.
- Foil hilt raised to the lips, then swept away to a low position.
- Mask on.

After saluting, you immediately move into the **On Guard** position. Turn to the next page for further details.

On Guard

On Guard is the *get ready* position for fencing (see Figure 20). When On Guard, you should be balanced and able to move forwards or backwards as necessary.

Figure 20: On Guard

REMEMBER!

When in the On Guard position, remember:

- Feet about shoulder width apart.
- Leading foot (sword arm side) at right angles to the rear foot.
- Both heels in line.
- Knees flexed.
- Body upright with shoulders parallel to the floor.
- Sword hand, elbow and shoulder in line.
- Back arm raised and relaxed.

Steps Forwards and Backwards_____

When fencing, it is important to move correctly. This allows you to change direction quickly, or attack or defend at any time, while constantly keeping your balance.

Figures 21 and 22 show a fencer moving forwards and backwards. In both illustrations, the dotted lines mark the position to which the fencer moves their leading or rear foot as appropriate.

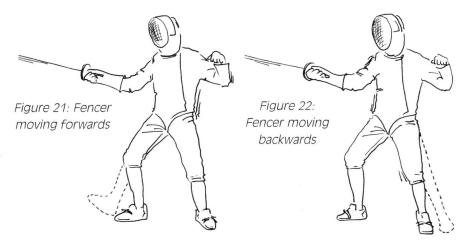

Figure 21: Fencer moving forwards

Figure 22: Fencer moving backwards

REMEMBER!

When moving forwards and backwards:

- Step forwards by moving your leading foot first and landing on your heel.
- Step backwards by moving your rear foot first and landing on the ball of your foot.
- Keep your knees flexed at all times.
- Don't drag your feet.
- Keep your feet the same distance apart.

Scoring a Hit

Scoring a hit means:

- placing the point of your foil on your opponent's target area accurately, without punching from your shoulder, and
- making the blade bend, so that if it were a sharp point, it would pierce the flesh.

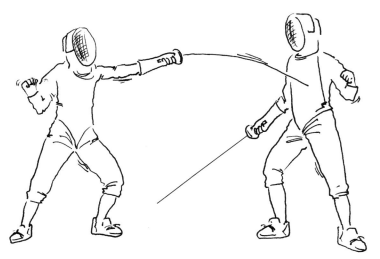

Figure 23: The fencer on the left is scoring a hit

When trying to score a hit, remember:

- Lower the point of your foil while extending your arm.
- Make sure the pommel finishes above the centre of your wrist.
- Keep your shoulder and elbow relaxed.

Lunge

Fencers normally keep at a distance from each other so that they cannot be hit by just an extension of their opponent's sword arm. To deliver a successful attack, you therefore need to **lunge** at your opponent while extending your sword arm to get close enough to score a hit. A lunge involves kicking forwards with the leading foot and driving forwards from the rear leg as shown in Figure 24 below.

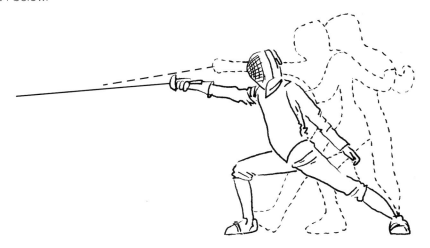

Figure 24: Attack with lunge

You must do this in such a way that you can:

- return to the On Guard position if your attack is unsuccessful
- recover forwards to continue the attack if your opponent moves backwards, or
- stay on the lunge *(not move)* to fence from that position.

REMEMBER!

To perform a lunge:

1 Begin extending your sword arm.

2 Simultaneously kick forwards with your leading foot and straighten your rear leg.

3 Extend your sword arm fully to maximum reach, with your hand just higher than your shoulder.

4 Position your leading knee vertically over your heel, with your body upright to keep your balance.

5 Throw your rear arm back.

To recover to the On Guard position:

1 Begin the recovery by bending your rear leg.

2 Bend your sword arm and lift your arm back as your leading foot recovers to the On Guard position.

Guards

A **guard** is a defensive/offensive blade position.

If you are holding your foil correctly and are also On Guard correctly, with your sword hand, elbow and shoulder in line, your opponent can only score a hit by attacking along one side of your blade. This is known as the **open line**.

Your opponent cannot see your target area on the opposite side of your blade. This is known as the **closed line**. In these circumstances, your blade position is known as a **guard**.

When you are in a guard, you should be able to hit your opponent by lowering the point of your foil and extending your sword arm in the normal way, without correcting your blade.

Types of Guards

There are eight guards, each numbered in Old French as follows:

1 **Prime**

2 **Seconde**

3 **Tierce**

4 **Quarte**

5 **Quinte**

6 **Sixte**

7 **Septime**

8 **Octave**

The target area in foil fencing is split into two halves, divided by an imaginary horizontal line at mid-chest height. The two halves are known as **high line** and **low line**. There are four high line guards and four low line guards.

Two high line (see Figures 26 and 28 overleaf) and two low line (see Figures 27 and 29 overleaf) guards are formed with the hand in a **pronated** position (knuckles pointing upwards) as shown in Figure 25 below.

Figure 25: Hand in pronation

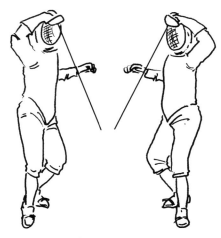

*Figure 26: Prime
(right- and left-handed versions)*

*Figure 27: Seconde
(right- and left-handed versions)*

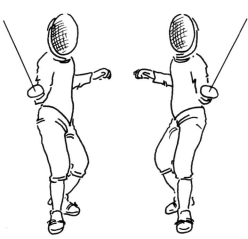

*Figure 28: Tierce
(right- and left-handed versions)*

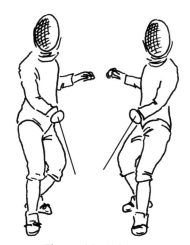

*Figure 29: Quinte
(right- and left-handed versions)*

Two high line (see Figures 31 and 32 opposite) and two low line (see Figures 33 and 34 opposite) guards are formed with the hand in a **semi-supinated** position *(thumb pointing upwards)* as shown in Figure 30 opposite.

Figure 30: Hand in semi-supination

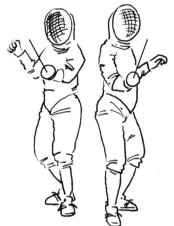

Figure 31: Quarte
(right- and left-handed versions)

Figure 32: Sixte
(right- and left-handed versions)

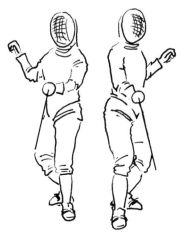

Figure 33: Septime
(right- and left-handed versions)

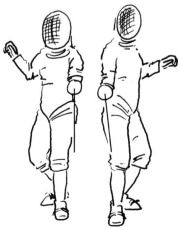

Figure 34: Octave
(right- and left-handed versions)

Defence

Parry

A **parry** is a defensive action made to ward off an attack.

If you adopt a guard during a bout, you can assume that your opponent will attack into an open line. To defend against the attack, you must deflect your opponent's blade with a parry. To do this, you must quickly move to another guard to close the line of attack and meet the **foible** *(flexible part of the blade furthest from the hilt)* of your opponent's blade with the **forte** *(half of the blade nearest the hilt)* of your blade.

Figures 35 to 42 show different types of parry that you can use.

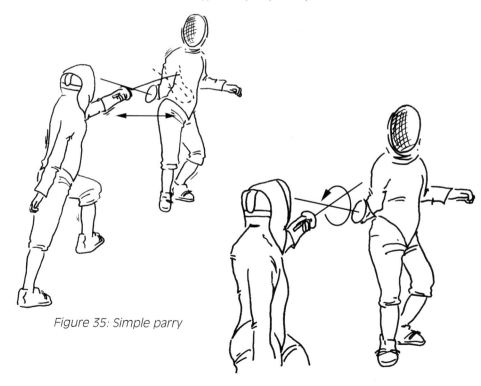

Figure 35: Simple parry

Figure 36: Circular parry of sixte

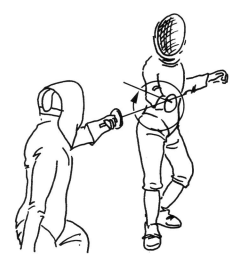

Figure 37: Circular parry of quarte

Figure 38: Semi-circular parry: from sixte to octave

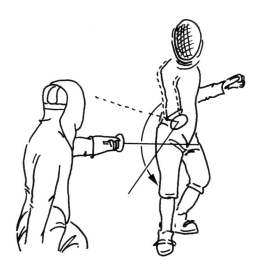

Figure 39: Semi-circular parry: from quarte to septime

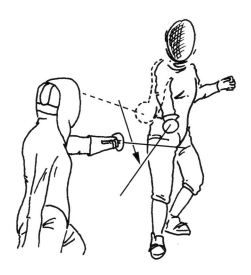

Figure 40: Diagonal parry: from sixte to septime

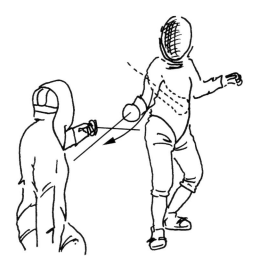

Figure 41: Diagonal parry: from quarte to octave

Figure 42: Prime parry

Riposte

A **riposte** is an offensive action that immediately follows a successful parry.

When your parry is complete, you can immediately hit back with a riposte. Your opponent must then defend and deliver a first **counter-riposte** as illustrated in Figure 43 below.

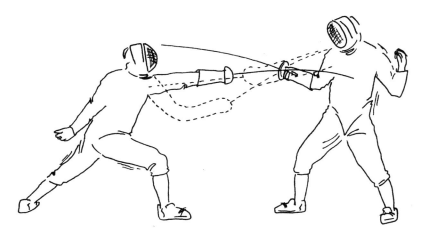

Figure 43: Counter-riposte

You can meet the first counter-riposte with a parry and second counter-riposte, and so on.

REMEMBER!

- A parry must finish in a guard.
- Do not move your feet when delivering a riposte unless your opponent recovers to the On Guard position or moves away.

Simple Actions_____

Simple actions are offensive actions made with only one blade movement. They can be either **direct** or **indirect**.

Direct Actions

A **direct attack** is an offensive action made without first passing over or under your opponent's blade and is known as a **straight thrust attack**. Figure 44 shows a fencer delivering a straight thrust attack.

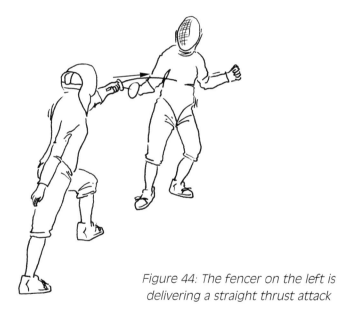

Figure 44: The fencer on the left is delivering a straight thrust attack

Both you and your opponent are free to deliver a straight thrust attack if:

* both of you adopt a guard and your blades are not in contact *(absence of blade)*, or

* neither of you is in a guard and your blades are in a low position.

This would also be the case following a successful parry when the attacking fencer would be open to a **direct riposte**.

Indirect Actions

An **indirect attack** is an offensive action made by first passing over or under your opponent's blade. It involves a *progressive* blade movement. This means you continue to extend your sword arm after passing over or under your opponent's blade to deliver the attack in one continual action.

There are two types of **indirect** attack as shown in Figures 45 and 46. In both illustrations, the dotted lines show the fencer's starting position and the arrows the direction in which the fencer moves their foil to attack their opponent.

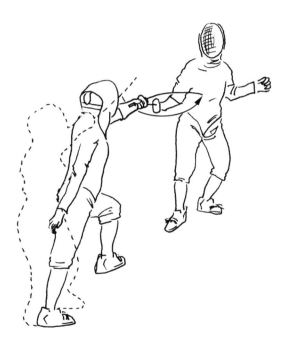

*Figure 45: Attacks that pass **under** the opponent's blade are known as **disengage attacks***

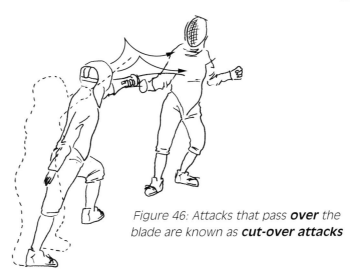

*Figure 46: Attacks that pass **over** the blade are known as **cut-over attacks***

To attack successfully, you must deliver an indirect attack into the open line if:

- both you and your opponent try to adopt guards and your blades are in contact, or

- your opponent tries to close a line by:

    - touching your blade *(engagement of blades)*, or

    - passing under your blade and re-engaging on the opposite side *(change of engagement)*.

This would also be the case following a successful parry when the attacking fencer closes the line to a direct riposte.

See page 40 for further details on *engagement of blades* and *change of engagement*.

REMEMBER!

Indirect actions involve:

- minimum blade movement

- using your index finger and thumb to manipulate your foil

- progressive blade movement with lunge.

Compound Actions_____

It will take you far longer to complete a simple attack with a lunge than it will for your opponent to react with a parry. To gain extra time, you can exploit your opponent's attempt to parry by using one or more **feint** *(false)* attacks.

By delivering a feint attack, you draw your opponent's parry and deceive your opponent by finishing your attack in a different line. A **compound attack** therefore consists of two or more simple attacks performed together and may be *progressive*. This means continuing to extend the sword arm after delivering one or more feints to complete the final part of the attack in one continual action.

You can deliver either a **direct** or **indirect feint** to draw your opponent's parry and deceive your opponent by delivering an indirect attack that finishes in a successful hit. If necessary, feints can be performed with additional foot movements (eg step lunge).

Figures 47 to 49 show the different types of compound attacks you can deliver.

*Figure 47: A **one-two** is used to deceive a simple parry*

*Figure 48: A **doublé** is used to deceive a circular parry*

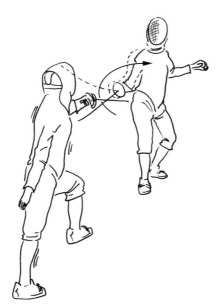

*Figure 49: A **low-high** is used to deceive a semi-circular parry*

It is also possible to deliver a **compound riposte** by using an indirect feint. The attacking fencer would be open to a compound riposte following a successful parry by their opponent.

Compound actions:

- involve minimum blade movement
- require realistic feint(s) to draw a parry
- can be progressive with a step(s) lunge.

Successive Parries

A **successive parry** consists of two or more consecutive parries made to defend against a compound attack. See page 34 for further details about compound attacks.

If your opponent delivers a feint to try to deceive your attempted parry, it follows that you will need to deliver a second parry to deflect the final part of your opponent's compound attack. These two defensive actions together form a successive parry.

To defend against a compound attack with more than one feint, you will need to deliver a number of successive parries to deflect the final part of your opponent's attack.

To deliver a successful compound attack, your opponent must try to predict which parries you will deliver. You are therefore more likely to defend successfully if you use a combination of different parries together. See pages 26–29 for details of the different types of parries.

To defend successfully against a compound attack, use combinations of different parries.

Tactics

Introduction

This chapter looks at tactics that can be used to gain an advantage over opponents. Starting with an explanation of why tactics are important, it then moves on to look at the tactical use of foot and blade actions, and concludes with a section on other tactics that can be used when fencing.

Like the previous chapter on key techniques, this chapter is specifically aimed at new fencers and therefore addresses the fencer as *you* throughout. However, coaches of new fencers will find it equally useful as an aid to developing fencers' tactical understanding of the sport.

Why are Tactics Important?

Foil fencing techniques are like a tool kit – they are not much use unless you know how and when to use them. Developing your tactical understanding of foil fencing requires a lot of practice.

To be a successful fencer, you need to be able to assess how to score a hit against your opponent and what your opponent is trying to do to prevent this. Similarly, you need to be able to assess how your opponent is scoring hits and what you need to do to prevent this.

Fencing is an *open skill* sport – you need to be able to perform actions correctly in constantly changing situations. For example, you may decide on a certain course of action, only to find that your opponent makes an unexpected blade or body movement. If this is the case, you will need to modify your course of action so as not to be caught out.

You will no doubt develop a preference for particular actions and may adopt a creative approach to the game. Generally, you may be more successful at attacking than defending. However, it is important to try to balance your strengths and weaknesses by training with a fencing coach.

Tactical Use of Foot Actions

The success of an attack or parry depends on the distance between you and your opponent. For example, if you deliver a simple attack from a distance where you need to lunge, your opponent will usually be able to react quickly enough to parry successfully. However, if the distance between you and your opponent is closer than lunging distance, your attack will be faster than your opponent's reaction to parry.

This section explains how foot actions can be used before and during attack to gain a tactical advantage over your opponent.

Before Attack

Step Forwards/Backwards Preparation and Lunge

To close the distance between you and your opponent and therefore gain a tactical advantage, you can precede a simple attack with a step forwards used as a **foot preparation**. However, if your opponent is trained to recognise such changes of distance, they will try to annul your advantage by stepping backwards to increase the distance again.

For you to deliver a successful attack, you will therefore usually need to immediately follow your step forwards preparation with a lunge. These two movements combined are known as a **step lunge**.

The same applies when performing a compound attack. If your opponent moves backwards while reacting to a feint, you must deliver your attack with a step(s) lunge.

Another way to gain a tactical advantage is to use a step backwards as a foot preparation and then immediately change to a step(s) forwards with lunge. By stepping backwards, you encourage your opponent to step forwards and therefore draw them into your planned attack.

If you are faced with an opponent who controls the distance between you and does not allow it to close, step forwards by closing the distance between your feet or crossing your feet as in a running step, and immediately follow this with a lunge. The same technique can be used to move backwards.

Second-intention

You can use a step forwards or backwards as a **second-intention**. This is an action made to provoke a reaction from your opponent that you can use to gain a tactical advantage. For example, you could step forwards to provoke an attack by your opponent in order to score a hit with a parry and riposte.

You can enhance a second-intention step forwards by performing a **jump forwards**, springing from your rear foot and landing with both feet together in an On Guard position. Similarly, you can enhance a second-intention step backwards by performing a **jump back**.

Appel and Balestra

The **appel** and **balestra** are sharp, stamping movements used to draw a reaction from the opponent, particularly when performing a feint attack.

- **Appel** – to perform an appel, stamp the ball of your leading foot. A rear foot appel is also possible.

- **Balestra** – to perform a balestra, make a short, sharp jump forwards so that you stamp the balls of both feet at the same time.

During Attack

To deliver a surprise attack on your opponent, use a **flèche** instead of a lunge. To perform a flèche:

1 Extend your sword arm and lean forwards as far as possible until you begin to lose your balance.

2 Spring forwards from your leading leg and drive the point of your foil forwards to your opponent's target area, allowing your rear leg to cross forwards as it follows through.

Figure 50 below shows a fencer performing a flèche.

Figure 50: Flèche

Tactical Use of Blade Actions

Blade actions can also be used before and during an attack to gain a tactical advantage over your opponent.

Before Attack

Engagement of Blades

An **engagement of blades** *(when both fencers' blades are in contact)* can be used to control your opponent's blade movement just before delivering an attack, particularly if used in conjunction with a step forwards. You can enhance the engagement by applying extra pressure to your opponent's blade just before releasing to attack.

If your opponent does not respond to the engagement, you can deliver a straight thrust attack. However, if they respond by pressing against the engagement or performing a **change of engagement** *(passing over or under your blade and re-engaging)*, you can deliver an indirect or compound attack.

If you attempt an engagement, this may provoke your opponent to deliver an attack on preparation and you may be able to score a hit with a parry and riposte.

Beat

A **beat** *(sharp striking of the opponent's blade)* can be used to:

- gain extra time to deliver a straight thrust attack, or

- provoke a return beat or parry by your opponent that will allow you to deliver an indirect or compound attack.

Change Beat

A **change beat** *(passing over or under the opponent's blade before beating)* can be used to confuse your opponent, particularly if used in conjunction with other blade preparations (eg change beat plus change of engagement with a step forwards).

Coulé and Froissement

An engagement of blades can be followed by a **coulé** *(grazing down the opponent's blade)* or **froissement** *(pressing forcefully while attacking)* before delivering an attack.

During Attack

Hits Made in Opposition

Certain blade positions, particularly engagements and parries in sixte and octave, can be followed by **hits made in opposition**. This means hitting while maintaining constant contact with your opponent's blade.

Prises de Fer

The **prises de fer** *(taking of the blade)* can be used while attacking or riposting to maintain control of your opponent's blade, particularly against a rigid, straight arm.

There are three types of prises de fer:

- **Bind** – the opponent's blade is engaged in a high line guard and carried diagonally into a low line guard, or vice versa.

- **Croisé** – the opponent's blade is engaged in a high line guard and carried into a low line guard on the same side, or vice versa.

- **Envelopment** – the opponent's blade is engaged in a guard and held in the same guard by a circular action of the attacker's blade under the opponent's blade.

See pages 23 to 25 for further information on high line and low line guards.

Tactics Within the Game

Timing

We have already seen how a tactical advantage can be gained by using certain foot and blade actions, but if these are used in the wrong circumstances, they are unlikely to be successful. For example, a compound attack will only succeed if your opponent tries to defend with the anticipated parry at the right moment.

The success of a particular action depends very much on *timing*. Your action may be *sympathetic* to your opponent's timing when trying to deceive your opponent's blade, or *contrary* to your opponent's timing to avoid being deceived when parrying, or by choosing the moment to attack as your opponent steps forwards.

Delivering a well-timed counter-attack into your opponent's attack can often stop the final part of your opponent's attack, or make their attack miss altogether. This is particularly effective if, while delivering your counter-attack, you:

- step forwards
- bring your feet together and lean backwards **(rassemblement)** as shown in Figure 51 below, or
- duck or move your body out of line as shown in Figure 52 on the opposite page.

Figure 51: Rassemblement

Figure 52: Counter-attack while ducking

Variation

Moving forwards and backwards at varying speed can help to catch your opponent off balance and create an opportunity to attack.

Varying the parries you use during a bout will make it more difficult for your opponent to anticipate them.

Remise and Redoublement

If you deliver an attack or riposte and your opponent parries, but does not riposte immediately, you can renew your attack by either pushing past the parry in the same line **(remise)**, or by passing around the parry to a different line **(redoublement)**.

Reprise

If you deliver an attack with lunge and your opponent moves away, you can perform a **forwards reprise**. This involves renewing your attack (either directly or indirectly, depending on your opponent's blade movements) by recovering forwards from the lunge into the On Guard position, keeping your sword arm straight and lunging again.

Similarly, you can perform a **backwards reprise** if your opponent moves towards you when you deliver an attack with lunge. This involves recovering backwards from the lunge into the On Guard position, keeping your sword arm straight and lunging again.

Flick Hit

The **flick hit** is an alternative method of scoring a hit. It involves flicking the point of the foil at your opponent and using the bend in the blade to score a hit on parts of your opponent's target area that are not exposed to a thrusting action (eg their back). In doing so, you have more chance of getting ahead of your opponent's parry. Before performing a flick hit, you need to close distance on your opponent and hold the point of your foil high, with your hand in pronation.

Figure 53 shows a fencer performing a flick hit to their opponent's back.

Figure 53: Flick hit to back

If you are right-handed and your opponent is left-handed (or vice versa), you are more likely to be successful if you direct hits:

• to the shoulder of your opponent's sword arm, or

• under your opponent's sword arm to the flank of their body as shown in Figure 54 below.

Figure 54: Hit to flank

This avoids the natural hazard of the opponent's sword arm that covers their chest area.

Teaching Fencing to Groups

Chapter 5

Introduction

This chapter is specifically aimed at coaches wishing to teach groups of new fencers and therefore addresses the fencing coach as *you* throughout. However, new fencers who are interested in finding out what goes on at fencing classes will find the chapter equally useful.

Subjects covered include:

- class safety
- class organisation
- dealing with equipment shortages
- fencing clubs
- coaching qualifications.

Class Safety

Local and education authorities generally regard fencing as a hazardous sport and you could be held responsible for any injuries resulting from unsafe or unsuitable activities. It is therefore your responsibility to ensure that fencing classes are conducted in a safe and enjoyable environment.

Fencing is actually one of the safest of sports, providing all equipment is in good condition and used sensibly. The only discomfort fencers are likely to suffer is the occasional bruise from an off-target hit, muscle cramp or stiffness. Follow the guidelines overleaf to make sure that all your fencing classes are safe ones.

Equipment

REMEMBER!

Never use a ...

- **foil** if the rubber button on the point is damaged. Tell your fencers to stop fencing and inform you immediately if the rubber button gets damaged or falls off

- **foil** with a broken or badly bent blade. Tell your fencers to stop fencing and inform you immediately if their foil blade breaks

- **mask** if the mesh caves inwards when pressed hard with the thumb

- **mask** showing signs of rust

- **mask** if the bib has become detached from the mesh or has any gaps or holes

- **jacket** that has tears or holes.

Always use ...

- proper fencing **jackets** that fasten at the back or on the non-sword arm side

- fencing **gloves** to protect fencers' sword hands. Make sure the cuff covers their jacket sleeve.

Safe Conduct

REMEMBER!

Never ...

- allow your fencers to use two hands to put their masks on when holding their foil

- allow your fencers to fool around with equipment

- leave a group unattended for any reason

- delegate responsibility for safety to an unqualified assistant or stand-in.

Always ...

- make your fencers aware of the potential hazards of mishandling their foils. Fencers must agree to use their foils responsibly before being allowed to fence

- hand out foils to fencers yourself – never allow them to help themselves

- ensure foils are carried by the pommel with the points down, except when fencing with full equipment

- ensure masks are fitted correctly before allowing your fencers to start fencing and make sure they know not to remove them before being instructed to do so by you

- identify unsafe practices, even if those involved are not under your direct control. The law recognises that coaches have a duty of care to ensure that all those who take part in fencing do so without endangering themselves or others.

Of course, accidents do sometimes happen. To avoid potential problems, make sure you are protected by public liability insurance and that you register your coaching qualifications with British Fencing. See page 53 of this handbook for further details about coaching qualifications and page 88 for British Fencing contact details.

Class Organisation

To run a fencing class, you will need a clear floor space about the size of a badminton court. There should be no more than 12 fencers to one coach in a class.

Explaining Fencing Techniques

When explaining fencing techniques, arrange your fencers in a line where they can see and be seen by you as shown in Figure 55 below.

Figure 55: A coach explaining fencing techniques

Remember, demonstrations are always better than descriptions.

Effective teaching involves:

Introduction

Demonstration

Explanation

Application.

Remembering the **IDEA** concept will ensure your fencers understand:

- **what** the technique is
- **why** they need to learn it
- **how** to perform the technique.

It may be necessary to break a movement down into parts if your fencers find it difficult to grasp the whole movement in one go. In these circumstances, demonstrate and explain each part of the movement.

Demonstrating Techniques with a Partner

If you want to demonstrate a fencing technique with a partner selected from the class, make sure your partner fully understands what to do before beginning the demonstration. If the demonstration involves using the foil, it is essential that both of you wear full safety equipment.

After the demonstration, you may well want to explain the technique to the rest of the class. In these circumstances, move well away from your partner before removing your mask. Alternatively, hold your partner's foil with your non-sword hand before removing your mask and talking, so that you keep complete control of the blade.

Practising Fencing Techniques

Once fencers move on to practising the fencing techniques you have taught them, split the class into pairs and arrange them in two rows, partners facing each other as shown in Figure 56 below. Make sure that all fencers are wearing full equipment.

Figure 56: A class practising fencing techniques

Ensure your fencers maintain correct basic positions during practices. Blade techniques should be practised in a stationary position at first, with speed and mobility being introduced as your fencers become more proficient.

Dealing with Equipment Shortages_____

Many key fencing techniques can be practised without using equipment. However, all new fencers will soon want to start using a foil. If you do not have enough equipment to go round, you will need to decide how to give all fencers a turn at using the equipment you do have.

If you can rely on your fencers to practise key techniques sensibly on their own, divide the class into two groups. One group can practise steps and lunges on their own without equipment while you supervise the other group using the equipment. Divide your lesson into periods and get the groups to change activities at the end of each period, so that they all have a turn at using the equipment.

If you are coaching a class of young fencers who cannot be left to themselves, start off by practising basic footwork together in one group without equipment. Then select a group of fencers to practise with the equipment, while the others watch until it is their turn. To avoid the fencers getting bored, keep each practice session short and rotate the groups regularly, so that everyone gets a turn at using the equipment.

Alternatively, you can practice with each fencer individually in a queue. After their turn, the fencer passes their equipment to the next person in the queue.

Under no circumstances should you distribute equipment to the whole class if it means fencers practising without a mask. Even if their partners are not using a foil, there is always the danger of them being hit in the eye by a careless classmate.

Fencing Clubs_____

Forming a fencing club can give a class, school or student group a real identity. Clubs affiliated to British Fencing receive lists of other fencing schools and clubs in the local area that matches could be arranged with, as well as details of local competitions. It is a good idea to appoint a club secretary and captain to be responsible for arranging matches, selecting teams, organising a club ladder and displaying fencing information on a club notice board.

Coaching Qualifications

If you are interested in coaching new fencers, it is recommended that you attend one of the many Club Leader courses organised throughout the country by British Fencing.

During this short course, you will receive training on:

- how to teach key fencing techniques correctly
- class organisation
- safe handling of equipment
- practical group teaching sessions.

On satisfactory completion of the course, you will receive a badge and certificate, and be registered on the National Register of Coaches. The qualification is recognised by local authorities as an indication of competence to teach fencing safely to new fencers of all ages.

Further coaching qualifications are available for club leaders who wish to improve their fencing knowledge and coaching skills. Full details can be obtained from British Fencing at the address given on page 88 of this handbook.

Chapter 6

Fencing Training

Introduction

Once fencers have mastered key fencing techniques, they need to learn to perform them correctly under the stress of competition. Fencing training should therefore involve performing fencing techniques under increasing levels of stress until they are performed well, even under the toughest of competitive conditions.

As with most other sports, the way to perfect fencing skills is through repetitive training exercises. Motivated, competitive fencers spend many hours doing training exercises to improve their performance, either by themselves, in groups, or individually with a coach. However, such repetitive training exercises can seem boring and demotivating. It is therefore vital to present them in as entertaining a way as possible.

There are various ways of improving fencers' coordination, concentration and perception. This chapter looks at how games, fun exercises and competitive exercises can be used to train new fencers. Like the previous chapter, it is specifically aimed at coaches wishing to train new fencers and therefore addresses the fencing coach as *you* throughout. However, new fencers who are interested in finding out what goes on at fencing training sessions will find the chapter equally useful.

Preparation

New fencers may find that performing fencing movements results in aching legs and over-stretched muscles. To avoid major discomfort and possible injury, always start your training sessions with a combination of warm-up activities and stretching routines.

Warm-up Activities

Always bear in mind that people attend fencing classes for a variety of reasons (eg to improve health and fitness, to make new friends, to escape from the stresses of everyday life). Warm-up activities help to create an enjoyable and sociable environment for the class.

Simple games with a soft ball, such as dodge ball or handball, encourage group interaction and allow everyone to participate to the best of their ability. Avoid activities to improve speed, strength and endurance with classes of new fencers.

Not only do warm-up activities help to create an enjoyable environment, they also increase the heart rate and prepare fencers for the stretching routine that follows.

Stretching Routines

The main fitness component required for fencing is **flexibility** *(the ability of joints to operate over their full range)*. For example, the length and speed of lunges rely on flexibility in the hips and the On Guard position relies on flexibility in the trunk and strength in the thighs.

Joint movement is limited by the lack of stretch in the muscles controlling the movement. To improve the range of movement in each joint, it is therefore necessary to stretch those particular muscles.

Include the following basic stretches in your routine:

Figure 57: Shoulder stretches

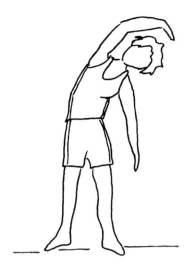

Figure 58: Side stretch

Figure 59: Trunk twist

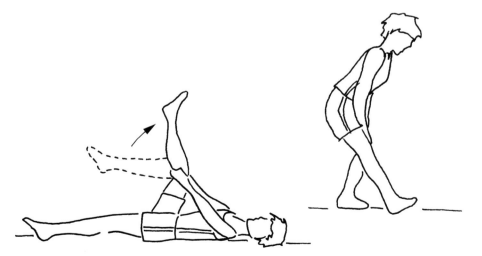

Figure 60: Hamstring stretches

Figure 61: Quads stretch

Figure 62: Hip flexor stretch

Figure 63: Inner thigh stretch

REMEMBER!

- Stretches should be performed slowly while breathing normally.
- Each stretch should be held for about 20 seconds or so.
- Each stretch should be repeated three times on each side of the body.
- Remind fencers not to overdo it and to stretch only as far as feels comfortable. They should feel the pull on their muscles, but not experience any pain.
- Explain the benefits of correct physiological exercise and encourage fencers to practise specific stretching routines on a daily basis.

Training Exercises

By the end of the preparatory session, fencers should feel warmed-up and ready to concentrate on the training session ahead.

This section describes a number of training exercises that can be used to develop key fencing skills. Each exercise relates to a key fencing technique – with a little imagination, you can develop your own!

Signals given to the class during the exercises can be made by hand or arm movements, by clapping, or with a whistle or verbal commands. To make the exercises more competitive, fencers who make mistakes can be *penalised* by having to do a certain number of press-ups or sit-ups etc.

REMEMBER!

- Tailor your training sessions to the age and personality of your fencers. A mixed group of teenage fencers may feel self-conscious if they are made to do exercises and games more suited to young children.

- Make sure that children's training sessions include lots of short duration activities with plenty of rests and drinks in between, especially in hot weather.

On Guard (no equipment required)

Exercise One

1   Divide the class into pairs.

2   One fencer acts as the coach and corrects and improves their partner's On Guard position within a specified short period of time.

3   When the time is up, inspect all the On Guard positions. If a fencer is not in the correct position, that particular *coach* is penalised.

Exercise Two

1 Arrange the class in a line facing you.

2 Instruct the class to start jogging slowly, moving forwards or backwards as directed.

3 On your command, they must jump into a perfect On Guard position.

Exercise Three

1 Arrange the class in a line facing you.

2 Instruct the class to adopt the On Guard position.

3 On your command, all fencers must change to an On Guard position with the opposite hand (ie all right-handed fencers become left-handed and vice versa).

4 Repeat your command faster and faster, so that the fencers have to change positions more quickly.

Exercise Four

1 Arrange the class in a line facing you.

2 Signal with your right hand – all fencers must adopt a right-handed On Guard position.

3 Check and correct their positions, and ask them to return to a standing position.

4 Signal with your left hand – all fencers must adopt a left-handed On Guard position.

5 Check and correct their positions, and ask them to return to a standing position.

6 Repeat the exercise mixing left- and right-handed signals at random to try and catch the fencers out. Errors or bad positions are penalised.

Variations of this exercise include asking the class to:

- jog on the spot while waiting for the signal to adopt the On Guard position
- sit on the floor and jump up into the appropriate On Guard position when the signal is given.

Steps Forwards and Backwards
(no equipment required)

Exercise One

1 Instruct the class to select a line marked on the floor.

2 Instruct the class to adopt the On Guard position so that they are facing down the line with both the leading and rear foot on the line.

3 Tell the class to step forwards and backwards as directed, keeping their leading foot or rear heel on the line as appropriate.

Variations of this exercise include asking the class to:

• work in pairs with one following the instructions given by their partner

• perform the exercise with their eyes closed.

Exercise Two

1 Arrange the class in a line facing you.

2 Instruct the class to adopt the On Guard position and to keep distance with you (ie as you step forwards one step, the class must step backwards one step; as you step backwards one step, the class must step forwards one step).

3 Repeat the exercise using different combinations of number of steps and direction.

Exercise Three

1 Arrange the class in a line facing you.

2 Instruct the class to adopt the On Guard position.

3 On your command, the class must perform fast short steps or long slow steps forwards and backwards as appropriate.

Variations of this exercise include instructing the class to:

• perform combinations of steps

• make up their own combinations of steps.

Exercise Four

1   Instruct the class to jog slowly around the room.

2   On your command, the class must change from jogging to stepping forwards along one side of the circuit without slowing down, and then continue jogging. The transition from jog to steps forwards back to jog should be smooth and should not interrupt the flow of the circuit.

Variations of this exercise include asking the class to:

- jog slowly forwards, then turn to perform steps backwards in the same direction without slowing down

- jog slowly forwards and perform a mixture of steps forwards and backwards in the same direction as directed.

Lunging (no equipment required)

Exercise One

1   Divide the class into pairs.

2   One fencer acts as the coach and corrects and improves their partner's lunge within a specified short period of time.

3   When the time is up, inspect all the lunges. If a fencer is not in the correct position, that particular *coach* is penalised.

Exercise Two

1   Divide the class into pairs.

2   One fencer adopts the On Guard position.

3   Their partner stands slightly ahead on the fencer's sword arm side and links their fingers loosely with the fencer's sword hand.

4   The partner gently pulls the fencer's sword arm forwards to maximum extension.

5   The exercise is repeated. Sometimes during the extension, the partner gives the command 'Lunge!' and releases the fencer's sword hand. The fencer must continue to extend their sword arm and perform a perfect lunge.

Exercise Three

1 Divide the class into pairs.

2 One fencer adopts the On Guard position.

3 Their partner stands on the fencer's sword arm side and offers an open hand at about shoulder height and at a distance that can easily be reached by a relaxed extension of the sword arm.

4 As the fencer reaches to touch the open hand, their partner occasionally moves their hand away, maintaining the same height above the floor. The fencer must continue to reach for their partner's hand with a smooth lunge.

Exercise Four

1 Arrange the class in a line facing you.

2 Instruct the class to adopt the On Guard position and to keep distance with you (ie as you step forwards and backwards, the class must step forwards or backwards as appropriate to maintain the distance between them and you).

3 On your command, the class must lunge, recover and continue stepping forwards and backwards as appropriate.

4 Repeat the exercise, getting faster each time.

Exercise Five

1 Divide the class into pairs.

2 Instruct the class to adopt the On Guard position, facing their partner and at lunging distance apart.

3 One fencer steps forwards and backwards and their partner must step forwards or backwards as appropriate to maintain the distance between them.

4 Occasionally, the fencer lunges and recovers. Their partner must immediately reply with a lunge and recovery.

Guard Positions (full fencing equipment required)

Exercise One

If mirrors are available, get the class to check their own guard positions, both front and side views, to make sure their positions are correct.

Exercise Two

1 Arrange the class in a line facing you.

2 Instruct the class to adopt the On Guard position.

3 Instruct the class to adopt a specific guard position.

4 Check each fencer's position by grazing your foil blade down their blade in the closed line and checking for adequate cover.

5 Repeat the exercise, specifying different guard positions each time.

Exercise Three

1 Arrange the class in a line facing you.

2 Instruct the class to adopt the On Guard position and to keep distance with you.

3 Instruct the class to change guards periodically as you step forwards and backwards.

Games and Fun Exercises

Most children and young fencers will have a limited capacity for prolonged concentration and disciplined training. It is therefore sometimes necessary to develop fencing skills in a light-hearted game situation.

Try to end your class periods or training sessions with a game as a reward for a successful class or session. Many playground games can be adapted to incorporate fencing techniques and language. This section looks at a few examples.

Relay Races

Teams race each other by performing fencing steps forwards to a line and returning by performing fencing steps backwards. In addition, you can instruct each team member to perform a set number of perfect lunges when they reach the line before being allowed to return.

Simon Says

1 Arrange the class in a line facing you.

2 Instruct the class to adopt the On Guard position.

3 Instruct the class to perform certain fencing movements (eg 'Simon says step forwards', 'Simon says step backwards'). The class must ignore any of your commands that do not include the words 'Simon says'. Those who make mistakes or perform techniques badly are eliminated and must act as judges. The winner is the surviving fencer.

On the Piste/Off the Piste

1 Arrange the class in a line facing you.

2 Instruct the class to adopt the On Guard position.

3 Tell the class that they are now *on the piste*.

4 When you say 'Off the piste!', the class must jump forwards, still maintaining the On Guard position. If you then say 'On the piste!', the class must jump backwards, maintaining the On Guard position. Use the commands 'Piste!' (for 'On the piste!') and 'Floor!' (for 'Off the piste!') to make it easier for the class to distinguish between the two commands.

5 If the class is already on the piste, they must not respond to the command 'On the piste!'. Similarly, if the class is already off the piste, they must not respond to the command 'Off the piste!'. Those who make a mistake or do not maintain the On Guard position correctly are penalised.

Silent Steps Forwards

1 Arrange the class in a line facing you.

2 Instruct the class to adopt the On Guard position.

3 Position yourself on a line marked on the floor parallel to the fencers' line, about six or seven metres away.

4 Turn your back to the class and step forwards two or three paces from the line.

5 The class starts to move forwards with silent fencing steps. Pick a moment to turn around sharply. Anyone who is moving or has not stopped in the correct On Guard position, must return to the starting line.

6 The game continues until someone successfully reaches the finishing line.

Fencing Tag

1 Instruct the class to adopt the On Guard position throughout the game and advise them they can step forwards or backwards in any direction.

2 Select one class member to try to *tag* their classmates by using fencing steps to chase them and a lunge to *tag* them. Those who are successfully *tagged* then try to catch the others.

3 To make the game more difficult, limit the class to moving only on badminton or basketball court lines marked on the floor.

Competitive Fencing

Chapter 7

Introduction

Fencing is a fighting sport and most new fencers will soon want to start competing with their classmates. This chapter starts by showing how competitive fencing can be introduced into class sessions. It then moves on to explain the principles of fencing on a piste, with or without electrical apparatus, and concludes with a brief outline of how fencing matches and competitions are organised.

Free Play

Free play allows fencers to try out their skills against each other and is a good way of introducing new fencers to competitive fencing.

Actions performed by fencers during early attempts at free play are often wild and uncontrolled. To ensure class safety, it is best to arrange the class in two rows facing each other as in pairs training (see Figure 56 on page 51 for further details).

Before free play, fencers must salute each other. Coaches must ensure that all fencers are wearing jackets, masks and gloves correctly. It is essential that no masks be removed until the whole class is instructed to stop fencing.

During free play, fencers can move forwards and backwards as necessary, but must not move sideways, circle each other or change sides.

Using the fencing techniques they have learnt, fencers try to score hits on their partners and must acknowledge hits scored by their partners. When a fencer scores a hit, whether on or off target, both fencers must stop fencing, return to their original starting positions and start again.

Just as fencing etiquette requires all fencers to salute each other before crossing swords, so they are required to shake hands with their partners at the end of the fight, after removing their masks. As they will be wearing a glove on their sword hand and holding their foil, handshaking is done with the non-sword hand. Left-handed fencers with right-handed partners just have to do the best they can!

Fencing on a Piste

For more organised fights and matches, it is necessary to mark out a **piste** on the floor. The best way to do this is to use short lengths of sticking tape to mark intersections and corners.

A **referee** controls the fight and assesses *priority* (ie who makes the attack, who parries and ripostes etc). In addition, each fencer is watched by two **judges** who determine when hits are scored and whether they are valid or non-valid (ie on or off target). The judges stand at the opposite end of the piste to the fencer they are watching, one on either side. The other two judges stand in similar positions at the other end of the piste as shown in Figure 64 below.

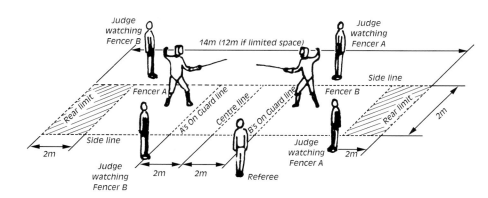

Figure 64: Fencing on a piste

Before the fight starts, both fencers must stand behind their respective On Guard lines. When the referee gives the command 'On Guard! Ready! Play!', both fencers must begin fencing, moving forwards and backwards on the piste as necessary.

The referee calls 'Halt!' when:

- one of the fencers scores a hit, whether on or off target
- there is an infringement of the rules, or
- the fencing becomes uncontrolled.

Generally, fencers must not cross the boundaries of the piste or change sides while they are fencing.

If one fencer is forced back until both feet cross the rear limit of the piste, a penalty hit is awarded to their opponent.

If one fencer crosses the side boundary of the piste with both feet, the referee calls 'Halt!'. The opponent is allowed to move forwards one metre while the offending fencer must move back the same distance. This may result in them crossing the rear limit of the piste and losing a penalty hit.

Scoring Hits

Each judge carefully watches their fencer and immediately raises a hand when they see a hit, whether valid or non valid. The referee calls 'Halt!', describes the **phrase** *(an exchange of actions performed without a break)* that led to the hit and asks each judge in turn their opinion on the hit.

Judges must reply:

- 'Yes' when they see a good hit made on target
- 'No' when the hit misses or is not made with the foil point
- 'Off target' when they see a hit made on a non-valid target, or
- 'Abstain' when they do not see the hit or they are not sure if it was on or off target.

Judges must always give honest opinions.

EXAMPLE

1 Fencer A attacks; Fencer B parries and ripostes; Fencer A parries with a counter-riposte.

2 The two judges watching Fencer B raise their hands.

3 The referee calls 'Halt!', describes the phrase that led to the hit and asks the judges watching Fencer B whether Fencer A's attack was successful: they both say 'No' (Fencer A's attack was successfully parried).

4 The referee asks Fencer A's judges whether Fencer B's riposte was successful: they both say 'No'.

5 The referee returns to Fencer B's judges, who still have their hands raised, and asks them whether Fencer A's first counter-riposte was successful: they both say 'Yes'.

6 The hit is awarded to Fencer A.

Each time a valid hit is scored, both fencers must return to their respective On Guard lines. The referee then restarts the fight, always giving the command 'On Guard! Ready! Play!'.

Disagreements

If two judges watching the same fencer disagree with each other, the referee may overrule one of them. However, if both are in agreement, the referee cannot overrule them.

If a judge or referee cannot decide whether a hit was on or off target, they must abstain from voting.

If two judges disagree on a particular hit and the referee abstains, or all three abstain, no hit is awarded.

Further Information

Full details on refereeing, judging and the rules for fencing on a piste is given in the Fédération Internationale d'Escrime (FIE) rule book. This can be obtained from British Fencing (see page 88 for contact details).

Fencing with Electrical Apparatus_____

For fencing competitions, judges are replaced by electrical recording apparatus that registers hits scored on both fencers.

Fencers wear **lamé jackets** *(metallic, woven-thread jackets covering the target area)* over their normal fencing clothing, and use foils with spring-loaded compression buttons.

A **body wire**, worn under the fencers' clothing, connects the foil to a spool with a retractable wire positioned at the end of the piste. This in turn is connected by floor leads to the recording box, which has red, green and white lights. Figure 65 below shows how the electrical apparatus is set up.

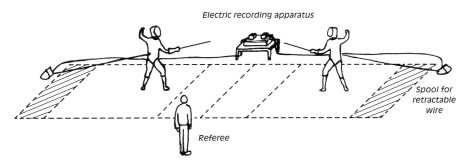

Figure 65: Fencing with electrical apparatus

If one fencer hits the other on their metallic jacket with the point of the foil, with sufficient force to depress the sprung button (500 grams), a coloured light shows on the recording box (one fencer is connected to the red light, the other to the green) and a buzzer sounds. If the hit is off target, the white light shows and a buzzer sounds.

The referee controls the fight in the same way described in the previous section (see pages 68 to 70), but refers to the lights on the recording box rather than judges to determine whether hits scored are valid or non-valid.

Fencing Matches and Competitions_____

Pool Sheets

During a competitive match or competition, the referee or scorer records all hits on a pool sheet as shown in Figure 66 below:

Event **REGIONAL FOIL CHAMPIONSHIPS**					**RND 1**				Pool No **2**			
Names	Nos	1	2	3	4	5	6	7	Total wins	Hits scored	Hits recd	Place
I. JONES	1	■	V (IIII)	V (IIII)	V (IIII)	2 (II)	3 (III)		3/5	20	18	+2 3
N. PAYNE	2	3 (III)	■	4 (IIII)	V (IIII)	V (IIII)	2 (II)		2/5	19	20	-1 4
E. FARRINGTON	3	2 (II)	V (IIII)	■	V (IIII)	3 (III)	2 (II)		2/5	17	22	-5 5
M. LAING	4	3 (III)	3 (III)	3 (III)	`	2 (II)	V (IIII)		1/5			6
J. HARRIS	5	V (IIII)	2 (II)	V (IIII)	V (IIII)	■	V (IIII)		4/5	22	14	+8 1
L. CLARK	6	V (IIII)	V (IIII)	V (IIII)	4 (IIII)	2 (II)	■		3/5	21	17	+4 2
	7							■				

Order of Assaults **4 PROMOTED TO RND 2**   Signature of president

Pool of 4	Pool of 5	Pool of 6		Pool of 7		Team of 3	Team of 4	
1–4	1–2	1–2	5–3	1–4	3–1	6–2	3–8	1–6
2–3	3–4	4–5	1–6	2–5	4–6	3–4	4–6	3–5
1–3	5–1	2–3	4–2	3–6	7–2	5–1	1–7	2–8
2–4	2–3	5–6	3–6	7–1	3–5	4–2	2–5	4–7
3–4	5–4	3–1	5–1	5–4	1–6	1–6	6–3	5–1
1–2	1–3	6–4	3–4	2–3	2–4	3–5	8–1	6–2
	2–5	2–5	6–2	6–7	7–3	1–4	5–4	7–3
	4–1	1–4		5–1	6–5	2–5	7–2	8–4
	3–5			4–3	1–2	6–3		
	4–2			6–2	4–7			
				5–7				

Leon Paul

Figure 66: Example of a pool sheet

Reproduced with the kind permission of Leon Paul Equipment Co Ltd

Each fencer's name is noted in the left-hand column of the pool sheet and they are allocated a number in the pool.

All hits scored by each fencer are recorded by drawing small dashes in the row next to their name. The vertical columns have corresponding numbers and indicate the hits scored by the fencer's opponent.

The order of fights for various pool sizes is shown at the bottom of the pool sheet.

Generally, all fights in the pool last for five hits. In competitions however, once the pool rounds have been completed and fencers move on to the later stages of the competition, fights last for 15 hits. See below for more information about fencing competitions.

Team Matches

In team matches, there are usually three fencers per team. One team occupies pool numbers 1 to 3 and the opposing team pool numbers 4 to 6. All members of one team fence all members of the opposing team, making nine fights in total. The team that wins the most fights wins the match.

Competitions

Competitions are organised on a knock-out basis. All fencers are grouped into first round pools (usually pools of six or seven fencers). Each fencer fights all the other fencers in their pool. The first fencer to score five hits wins the fight.

A number of fencers are eliminated after the first round. The remaining fencers are seeded and drawn against an opponent. The first fencer to score 15 hits wins the second round; their opponent is eliminated from the competition.

Winners of the second round move onto further rounds. Fencers are gradually eliminated until there is one final winner.

Glossary of Fencing Terms

Absence of blade	When swords are not in contact.
Advance	To step forwards.
Aids	The last three fingers of the sword hand.
Analysis	The process of describing actions occurring in a fight, usually a phrase leading to a hit.
Angulation	Pronating or supinating the sword hand and flexing the wrist, so creating an angle between the weapon and the sword arm.
Annulment of hit	A valid hit which is disallowed because of an infringement of rules or a technical fault.
Appel	Beating the piste with the ball of the foot, either as a *front foot* or *rear foot* appel.
Arm judges	Two judges appointed by the referee to watch both fencers for illegal use of the rear arm.
Arrêt	*See* **Stop hit**.
Assault	Combat between two fencers.
Attack	An initial offensive action made by extending the sword arm and continuously threatening the opponent's target area.
Avoidance	Ducking or moving sideways to avoid being hit.
Balestra	A short, sharp jump forwards, usually used as a preparation.
Barrage	A fight-off to determine a result in the event of a tie.
Beat	A crisp, striking action with the blade on the opponent's blade to create a deflection or stimulate a reaction.

Bib	Soft, padded section of the mask to protect the neck and throat.
Bind	Taking of the foible of the opposing blade diagonally from high to low line, or vice versa.
Blade	The main component of a sword on which the hilt is mounted.
Body wire	Wire worn under a fencer's clothing to connect the sword terminal to the retractable spool cable, when using electrical apparatus.
Bout	A fight for a specific number of hits.
Breaking ground	Stepping back.
Breeches	White, knee-length trousers made from robust material; the side fastening must be on the non-sword arm side and the legs must fasten below the knees.
Broken time	A pause introduced into an action that is normally performed in one continuous movement.
Brutality	Actions performed with an unacceptable level of force or violence that causes discomfort to the opponent.
Button	Soft covering for a non-electric foil point.
Cadence	The rhythm in which a sequence of movements is made.
Ceding parry	A parry formed by giving way to the opponent's prises de fer.
Change beat	A beat made after passing under or over the opponent's blade.
Change of engagement	Re-engagement of the opponent's blade after passing over or under it.

Chest protectors	Rigid breast cups which are worn inside women's fencing jackets *(individual)* or a rigid breast plate which is worn underneath women's fencing jackets *(full)*.
Choice of action	A predetermined action performed when conditions are suitable.
Choice reaction	A reasoned response to a change of conditions presented by the opponent.
Circular parry	A parry formed by making a circle with the foil point under the opponent's blade, so deflecting the opponent's attack into the closed line.
Close quarters	When two fencers are close together, but can still wield their weapons.
Competition	Aggregate of individual bouts or team matches required to determine a winner.
Compound action	Two or more single actions performed together as one continuous action.
Compound attack	An attack comprising one or more feints.
Compound prises de fer	Two or more consecutive takings of the blade without loss of blade contact.
Compound riposte	A riposte comprising one or more feints.
Conventions	Rules governing the priority of attack.
Coquille	Bell-shaped guard of a foil.
Corps à corps	Bodily contact between fencers during a bout.
Coulé	Grazing lightly down the opponent's blade while extending the sword arm, maintaining sword contact throughout.
Counter-attack	An offensive action made while avoiding or closing the line against an opponent's attack.

Counter-disengage	An indirect action that deceives a change of engagement.
Counter-offensive action	*See* **Counter-attack**.
Counter-parry	*See* **Circular parry**.
Counter-riposte	A riposte following the successful parry of the opponent's riposte or counter-riposte.
Counter-time	An action made by the attacker into a provoked counter-attack.
Coupé	*See* **Cut-over**.
Croisé	The taking of the foible of the opposing blade from high to low line, or vice versa, in the same line as the engagement.
Crosse grip	A moulded grip with finger protrusions.
Cross steps	Running steps forwards or backwards.
Cut-over	An indirect action made by passing the blade over the opponent's blade.
Defence	Not being hit by the opponent's attack either by parrying, avoiding or moving out of distance.
Delayed	Actions made after a pause.
Dérobement	Evasion of the opponent's attempt to beat or take the blade while the sword arm is straight and the point is threatening the target area.
Detachment	When both blades break contact.
Development	Extension of the sword arm accompanied by a lunge.

Glossary of Fencing Terms

Diagonal parry	Deflecting the opponent's attacking blade by moving from a high line guard to a low line guard on the opposite side, or vice versa.
Direct	Actions made without passing over or under the opponent's blade.
Direct elimination	Method of competition organisation where winners are promoted to the following rounds and losers are eliminated after one fight.
Disciplinary code	Fencers who agree to take part in fencing pledge their honour to observe rules of competition and respect the decisions of officials.
Disengagement	An indirect action made by passing under the opponent's blade.
Displacement	Turning or ducking to remove the valid target area from its normal position.
Disqualification	Elimination from a competition due to cheating or bad behaviour, or by default etc.
Doublé	A compound attack that deceives the opponent's attempted circular parry.
Double action	When both fencers choose exactly the same moment to make an offensive action.
Draw	Seeding of fencers to determine the bouts in a competition.
Duration of bout	Actual fencing time allowed during a bout. A stopwatch is started at the beginning of a bout and stopped each time the referee halts the fencers. It is restarted when the referee says 'Play!'

Glossary of Fencing Terms

Earthing of guard	Guards of electric weapons must be earthed correctly so that point hits do not register on them.
Earthing of piste	Metal pistes must be correctly earthed so that point hits do not register on them.
Electrical apparatus	An electric box with red and green lights to register valid hits and white lights to register non-valid hits. The apparatus is mounted centrally, adjacent to the piste, and connected by floor leads to spools with retractable cables placed at both ends of the piste, to which the fencers connect their body wires.
Electric weapons	Foils suitable for use with electrical apparatus.
Engagement	When both blades are in contact.
Envelopment	The taking of the foible of the opponent's blade by making a complete circle and maintaining continual contact throughout.
False action	An action made to assess the opponent's reaction or to provoke a reaction that can be exploited.
Feint	Threatening an attack to provoke a parry that can be deceived.
Fencing line	A theoretical straight line running through the leading feet of opposing fencers.
Fencing measure	The distance between two fencers such that they must lunge to score a valid hit.
Fencing position	The position adopted by a fencer to maintain a guard.
Fencing time	The time required to perform one simple fencing movement.
FIE	*Fédération Internationale d'Escrime* – the international governing body of fencing.

Glossary of Fencing Terms

Finger play	A method of manipulating the weapon with the index finger and thumb.
Flank	The side of the trunk of body on the sword arm side.
Flèche	Offensive movement made by leaning forward so as to cause a loss of balance.
Flick hit	An exaggerated throwing of the point to use the bend in the blade to register a hit with an electric foil.
Foible	The flexible half of the blade furthest from the hilt.
Foil (Fleuret)	Originally developed as a practice version of the small sword with a rectangular blade and blunted point.
Forte	The half of the blade nearest to the hilt.
French grip	The hilt style that has a slightly curved handle and pommel.
Froissement	Deflecting the opponent's blade by opposition of *forte to foible* while blades are engaged.
Gaining ground	Stepping forwards.
Glove	Protection for the sword hand, made of strong material with a cuff of sufficient length to reach halfway between the wrist and elbow.
Graze	*See* **Coulé**.
Grip (of weapon)	The handle part of the hilt.
Grip	The method of holding the weapon.
Guard (of weapon)	The part of the hilt to protect the sword hand.
Guards	Defensive/offensive blade positions. *See* **Prime, Seconde, Tierce, Quarte, Quinte, Sixte, Septime, Octave.**

High line — The target area above a theoretical horizontal line midway through the fencer's trunk of body.

Hilt — The assembled parts of the sword excluding the blade.

Hit — To strike the opponent with the point of the weapon in such a way that if the point had been sharp it would have pierced the flesh.

Immediate — An action made without a pause.

Indicators — A system used in competitions to determine a fencer's seeding after the first round. The first indicator is expressed as a ratio of the number of victories and the number of fights, and the second indicator is the number of hits scored, minus the number of hits received.

Indirect — An offensive action made by first passing over or under the opponent's blade.

Italian foil — A weapon which has a hilt with a guard and crossbar.

Jacket — A protective jacket covering the valid target area, made from robust material without fastenings on the front or the sword arm side.

Judges — In non-electric bouts, four judges watch for hits on both fencers (two per fencer).

Jury — The referee and four judges who officiate during a bout.

Jury d'appel — A group consisting of one representative from each nation taking part in a competition to which a fencer or team captain can appeal against a misapplication of the rules.

Glossary of Fencing Terms

Lamé jacket

A metallic, woven-thread over-jacket covering the valid target area which is worn when using electrical apparatus.

Low-high attack

A compound attack that deceives the opponent's attempted semi-circular parry.

Low line

The target area below a theoretical horizontal line midway through the fencer's trunk of body.

Lunge

A method of getting closer to an opponent with acceleration to make an attack, while maintaining balance and making it possible for a rapid recovery to On Guard.

Martingale

The loop of tape or leather attached to the grip and held to prevent a non-electric foil from flying out of the hand in the event of being disarmed.

Mask

Wire mesh covering worn on the head to protect the face, sides of the head and neck.

Octave

A low line, semi-supinated guard on the sword arm side.

One-two attack

A compound attack that deceives the opponent's simple parry.

On Guard

The *get ready* position in fencing.

Orthopaedic grip

A general term for moulded grips of various designs.

Parry

Defensive action to deflect an opponent's attack by opposing *forte to opponent's foible*.

Phrase

An exchange of actions performed without a break.

Piste

The field of play on which a bout takes place.

Plastron	A half-jacket with no underarm seam, worn under the fencing jacket for extra protection during competitions; also a padded over-jacket worn by fencing coaches when giving individual training.
Pommel	A metal cap screwed to the end of the foil hilt that locks the parts of the weapon together and provides a counterbalance weight to the blade.
Pool (Poule)	The grouping of fencers or teams in a competition.
Preparation of attack	The movement of the blade or foot to obtain the best position from which to make an attack.
Pressure	A pressing movement of the fencer's blade against an opponent's blade to deflect it, or cause a reaction.
Prime	A high line, pronated guard on the non-sword arm side.
Principles of defence	The execution of a parry by the defender's forte opposing the attacking foible *(ie opposition of forte to foible)*.
Priority	The right of way gained by the fencer who initially extends the sword arm, with the foil point continually threatening the opponent's target area.
Prises de fer *(Takings of the blade)*	*See* **Bind, Croisé, Envelopment**.
Progressive actions	Actions made with the foil point continually moving towards the opponent's target area.
Pronation	The position of the sword hand with the knuckles uppermost.
Quarte	A high line, semi-supinated guard on the non-sword arm side.
Quinte	A low line, pronated guard on the non-sword arm side.

Glossary of Fencing Terms

Rassemblement
: The bringing of both feet together, either forwards or backwards, with the body in an upright position, in order to outreach the opponent.

Reaction
: A response to a stimulus, either as a natural reflex action or as a developed reflex action.

Recovery
: The return to the On Guard position.

Redoublement
: The renewal of an action after being parried by replacing the point on the target area in a different line to the original action.

Referee
: The official who directs and controls a bout and awards hits.

Remise
: The renewal of an action after being parried by replacing the point on the target area in the line of the original action.

Renewals
: The continuation of the original offensive action following the opponent's successful parry.

Repechage
: The competition formula which gives losers of a direct elimination bout a second chance to stay in the competition.

Reprise
: The renewal of an action made with a lunge by first returning to the On Guard position, either forwards or backwards.

Retire
: To step back.

Riposte
: An offensive action immediately following a successful parry.

Salute
: The acknowledgement of respect shown to an opponent, fencing coach or training partner before crossing swords.

Seconde
: A low line, pronated guard on the sword arm side.

Glossary of Fencing Terms

Second-intention	An action made to provoke a movement from the opponent.
Semi-circular parry	The deflection of the attacking blade by making a semi-circle with the point of the foil, from high to low line on the same side or vice versa.
Semi-supination	The position of the sword hand with the thumb uppermost.
Sentiment du fer	The use of the tactile senses of the fingers of the sword hand, mainly the thumb and index finger, to give an awareness of the contact of blades.
Septime	A low line, semi-supinated guard on the non-sword arm side.
Simple attack	An offensive action made with one blade movement in one period of fencing time. May be direct or indirect.
Simple parry	The deflection of the attacking blade by moving the foil from sixte to quarte in the high line or vice versa, or septime to octave in the low line or vice versa.
Simultaneous attack	When both fencers choose precisely the same moment to make an offensive action.
Sixte	A high line, semi-supinated guard on the sword arm side.
Spools	Part of the electrical apparatus that has retractable cables to connect fencers to the electrical recording box.
Stance	The position of the feet and legs of the fencer while in the On Guard position.
Stop hit	A counter-offensive action into the opponent's attack.
Stop hit in opposition	A counter-offensive action that closes the line against the opponent's attack.
Straight thrust	A direct attack made in one line.

Successive parries	Two or more consecutive parries made to defend against a compound attack.
Supination	The position of the sword hand with the palm uppermost.
Taking of the blade (Prises de fer)	See **Bind, Croisé, Envelopment**.
Tang	The part of the blade on which the hilt is mounted.
Target area	The trunk of body, excluding the head and limbs. The limits of the target area are as follows:

- Upper limit – up to 6cm above the collar bones. The bib of the mask is not included in the target area.
- Side limit – to the seams of the jacket sleeves.
- Lower limit – to the V to the groin at the front of the jacket and the waist at the back of the jacket.

Tempo	The rhythm of movement which determines fencing time.
Temps d'éscrime	See **Fencing time**.
Tierce	A high line, pronated guard on the sword arm side.
Trompement	Deception of the opponent's attempt to parry.
Valid hit	A hit that arrives correctly on target.

British Fencing
1 Baron's Gate
33–35 Rothschild Road
London
W4 5HT
Tel: 020-8742 3032
Fax: 020-8742 3033
E-mail: british_fencing@compuserve.com
Website: www.britishfencing.com

sports coach UK
114 Cardigan Road
Headingley
Leeds
LS6 3BJ
Tel: 0113-274 4802
Fax: 0113-275 5019
E-mail: coaching@sportscoachuk.org
Website: www.sportscoachuk.org

Patron: HRH The Princess Royal

For over 400 carefully selected sports-related
products contact us for your free catalogue
or log onto our website:

Coachwise 1st4sport
Coachwise Ltd
Chelsea Close
Off Amberley Road
Armley
Leeds LS12 4HP
Tel: 0113-201 5555
Fax: 0113-231 9606
E-mail: enquiries@1st4sport.com
Website: www.1st4sport.com